Wild Blue Yonder

A collection of poems
and creative
invitations

Leah Campbell Badertscher

To all you out there who want to bring your dreams off the page, your imagination out of the capture of limitations and into the wild blue yonder...off we go!

To Deb and Boyd.
Thank you with all my heart and being. Because of you, all things are possible. I love you.

Contents

Part Two: Creative Prompts

Foreword

When I was a little girl, I'd climb into the front seat of my Grandma Donna's old blue Buick and buckle up for an adventure. Plush blue seats, hot silver seat belt with a gem-like button in the middle that I'd click in, she'd shift the car into gear, gravel crunched beneath the tires as we pulled out of the drive of our family farm and onto the country road. Once we picked up some speed, she'd pound the dash with exuberance and launch into song,

"Off we go, into the wild blue yonder! Flying high, into the sun!"

And off we'd go, up and down dusty country roads looking for beauty. Beauty in the horizon, in the changing colors of the sky, beauty in the ditch flowers, and the birds that loved them.

No longer flat, fly-over territory, it was a runway for taking off into the Wild Blue Yonder.

A ride in the car with my grandmother and I could see the world in a different way; *I could see it as an artist.*

Seeing the world, experiencing the world as an artist is what I believed awakened the seed in me–*I am an artist.*

Those simple, humble adventures on backcountry roads and into the Wild Blue Yonder helped me to see and experience something profound. The Wild Blue Yonder was a version of reality, of life, that I touched, was something where a truth of a reality in me, an expansive, wondrous one, touched and connected with a truth of the world out there – one full of endless possibility and exciting discoveries!

My journey to becoming an artist, though, did not mirror the arc of that old military tune, "Off we go, into the wild, blue yonder!" My path was not linear or one of flying high and then just soaring off into the horizon as a fully hatched, fully realized, artist. That girl that loved creativity, imagination, beauty, art was always there, but for years she took a back seat, while a different part of me took a different tour; one that included a finance degree and then becoming a lawyer.

It would be many years after those car rides with my Grandma Donna before that seed, *I am an artist* would start to crack through.

One of those cracks for me occurred in law school when she passed away. I inherited boxes of her art supplies. When going through them, I found some of her journals. They would begin with her writing down some of her wonderful tales, or jotting down descriptions of art she wanted to create, but then the voice of the creative spirit, my grandmother's feisty and exuberant voice that I knew so well, would begin to trail off and be choked out by this other voice. A voice of self-doubt, fear, and self-judgment. They were all half-complete.

My heart was broken, but I knew that was a gift. I promised not to waste this heartbreak, knowing that this woman I loved so dearly and who was a great champion to my creativity had left me a final lesson, and it would not be lost on me. I vowed, "no more half-finished journals! No more creative dreams oppressed by the violence of self-doubt and self-criticism!"

That heartbreak helped crack open that artist seed in me, and I began to nurture it on purpose. That was almost 20 years ago. In that time, over the course of several years, I've become a working artist who creates art that I love and that I love for other people to love. I also have sold those paintings for thousands of dollars.

I've also done a lot of writing over the past several years. Something has been tugging on my soul, though. While much of my work I do share with the world, my own poetry and stories still mostly live on the pages of my personal journals or on my hard drive.

I'd like a little more time. I'd like to be better at this before I share it. Something in me tells me I'd be better off with a little more thought, a little more polish, a little more time. But I think I can hear my grandma calling. If I listen and try just a little, I can even see her standing outside her car, motioning me to come towards her, saying, "Hey, sweetheart. It's time. Want to go for a ride?"

In addition to being an artist and writer, I have also built a very successful creativity coaching career as a master life coach, and am passionate about building a paradigm of thriving artists. My clientele make up both working, professional artists of all genres and those with more traditional careers who desire to carve a more authentic path for themselves. What all of my clients tend to share in common, though, is a desire to unleash their creativity and to be a creative force of nature, being the most powerful leaders of their own lives, and creating success on their own terms, aligned with their values, from the inside-out.

In 2018, I founded that which I found myself longing for on my own creative journey, The Art School. The Art School is a program that imparts my philosophy that by cultivating an extraordinary way of being, in mind, body, and spirit, the extraordinary results we dream of creating flow inevitably from who we are. Through teaching workshops, mentoring and coaching individuals, and through my podcast, The Art School Podcast, I am working to help build a paradigm of thriving artists and creatives because I know that fully empowered, expressed, thriving creatives not only can create better lives for themselves, but they are also essential for building a better world.

One of my core beliefs is that "*everybody has an in.*" One of the worst feelings I have experienced is to have a desire to create something and to feel like I was stuck, like I was in my own way and not capable of bringing this creative vision to life. Fortunately, it was an intense enough of an unpleasant experience that I was sure there must be a better way and a better experience of being a creative and I was resolved to find it! Turns out, there was a better way (it's something I refer to as "The Third Way" with my students) and there is a better experience of being creative (and to me, I can often sum it up as that "Wild, Blue Yonder" feeling or, simply, the feeling of being Fully Alive!).

Through the process of healing my own creative spirit, I sought out teachers, mentors, artists I looked up to, and coached myself to unleash my creative. I also, at one point, made a life-changing decision—that I have a wise, inner guardian within me, that that is actually what creative genius means to me, and I could rely on this to guide. Leaning into this trust, I was able to intuitively find ways to use my own imagination to guide me.

This book includes several of my own poems as well as prompts you can give to your own imagination to unleash your own creative genius and bring your art to life! It occured to me later in the process of editing this book that publishing the poetry is also a prompt in the way of an example. Therefore, this entire book is both a creative work while also being an example and invitation to you of how you might discover your own path to liberated, thriving creative expression in your chosen mediums, as well as your unique creative, extraordinary way of living that helps you break through to your own "Wild, Blue Yonder," and feels your life with the energy of being fully alive. In the spirit of that, I want to share some of the fruits of that process, my poetry, with you. I also wanted to share some of my process and "the how-to," in case you find yourself in need of a breakthrough you now and then, whether specifically in your own art form or in life.

I hope you enjoy this book, may it help you in discovering your own Third Way and lead to many meaningful creative breakthroughs. Maybe I'll even get to meet you and your creative work someday!

Until then, off we go! Into the wild, blue yonder...

With love,

Leah

"The world was made to be free in..."

DAVID WHYTE

"I love my creative life more than I love cooperating with my own oppression."

CLARISSA PINKOLA ESTES

"Off we go, into the wild blue yonder!"

LYRICS FROM 1939 "ARMY AIR CORPS," OFTEN SUNG BY DONNA ANDRESEN CAMPBELL

Tiny Poem from The Big Water

You, standing there on the brink,
growing more parched every moment
you spend contemplating
the deep swim.

Don't content yourself to drink
from a glass
just because everyone else
sips neatly from their thimbles.

Dive in!

Lose your-self in Me.

Looking for Cracks

There are days I must find the cracks.

There are days I must find the cracks,
must dig my fingers into whatever crack I can find
(it is rarely an obvious or overly generous opening,
most often it's just an ordinary, stingy little fissure,
hardly seeming adequate to accomplish the task of
opening a portal to another world...)

On these days when I cannot see houses to warm-blooded people,
when I cannot stretch the imagination of my heart to appreciate
that those tall shorn tree stumps bring and bear light
and warmth to many and where the miracle once made its way slow
as sap
through their veins,
now they carry veins that allow another miracle to zip along those
lines...

On these days when I feel the world, however well-intentioned and
well-suited
for so many others, just seems to be choking me out,
when everything that is anything to anyone else is artificial to me
and obstructs the wide and clear blue sky and blocks the horizon...

I want to dig my fingers into the crack and pry apart this world,
Ripping it back at the seams,
Revealing what is underneath.

I want to unhinge the busy landscape and release a wide, clear sky.
I want to rip apart the noise and plunge into the silence.
I want to find a crack somewhere between
house, yard, fence,
fence, yard, house,
between the electrical poles and the concrete sidewalk and parked
cars,
I want to dig my fingers deep into that crack and pry apart this
unnatural,
This alien world,
And live in the one beneath. Beneath the breath.

On these days, when you find yourself so certain that this is not real,
(there must be more to life?! To me?!)

begin looking for the seams.

Run your eyes, your mind, your fingers, your imagination along the
edges of everything that you think you know, and question and feel.
Question and Feel, feel and question, and wonder, and pause, and
feel, until you find the seams. Run your fingers along the seams until
you find the crack,

Something you can pry your fingers into...

Maybe a tiny split where one neighbor's fence meets the other
neighbor's lawn...

Maybe between the electrical poles and concrete sidewalk and parked cars...

Find the cracks, pry your fingers into any opening with a little give...
anything that seems both familiar and foreign, unquestioned and
unnatural, accepted and alien...

And begin to dig until you find the world beneath the world.

But what if you find yourself in a glass terrarium,
and there are no cracks in its smooth walls?
You can see freedom, you just can't live there.
Throw everything you've got at it. Make a crack.

The Cricket

The cricket came first
in a white box.

I asked the Muse to deliver something! Anything!
Surprise me! I said.

She (strangely appearing as St. Michael the Archangel)
handed me a small white box.

It was the size that could have held a piece of quartz,
a baseball,
or a human heart.
One time it held a lemon,
but this time I removed the lid to see
one lone, black cricket.

After that, I began to see crickets everywhere,
even places unexpected.
On a walk a beautiful crimson leaf, gilt around the edges,
caught my eye as it lay on the sidewalk.
I picked it up to reveal yet another cricket underneath.

In the early mornings as I sat in my living room chair next to the

window,
trying to write as they chirped at me.
I looked inside and outside the house and couldn't find them,
but still they chirped away.

Because the crickets would neither say more or less,
I asked the Muse for something again—

This time (The Muse appearing this time as the Winged Victory of Samarathrus-
though this one, unlike her unfortunate sister in the Louvre, was not of stone
and still had her head)
she handed me

The same white box.
And another black cricket.

So, I decided my job was to listen.

Now, when the moon pulls me out of bed
(always at that same 2:30 AM slant in the sky)

I listen to the crickets.

I listen with my ears,
I listen with chambers in my heart,
I try to listen with faculties I don't even have yet...

I've been listening since early August,
and now it's mid-October,

Their song has changed,

they're singing now from that
cold is approaching harvest hymnal,

I'm straining to understand before
the frost coats their black armor and winter's lullabye
sings them to sleep...

Their song...
It has something to do with the stars,
that I can decipher,
something with their music
the symphony of chirps
is unraveling the meaning of
the spinning of galaxies
far away

But that, too, fades from me and now...

I wake and this morning
A hard frost.

I listen and still don't know what was meant
by their music,
only that it was here and it Is now gone.

Adonus Drives for Uber

ADONUS will arrive
in two minutes
in a Chrysler 200

Well, I thought,
this should be interesting.

Adonus arrived,
a thirty-something black man (or so he appeared)
in a silver Chrysler
with silver wings on the back of the trunk.

Surely an Adonus
has a story to tell,

Surely I should just
shut up and listen, I thought.

He first unfolded a tale
of waking at three a.m.

Of the fog of exhaustion
that descends

like clockwork
every morning at 6:10,

Of the discipline
it takes to fight the urge
to go home
to fight the urge to sleep.

How many days do you drive? I asked
Six, he said.

How many hours a day? I asked
As many as it takes, he said.

I could tell by the way he said,
As many as it takes,

that "takes to what?" was none of my business.

But still, he was not unfriendly—and
I sensed a story in him.

Something I was meant to hear.

Something, even, that he,
messenger,
Adonus that drives for Uber,
wanted me to know.

So I asked a different question:

"What do you like to do when you're not driving?"

Coach basketball, he said,
I absolutely love to coach basketball.

And the way he said it—
I knew he had given me something.

I always knew I wanted to coach,
so when the youngest of my five went to college,
I did.

I wondered if he knew the
Story of Adonis,
Of Aphrodite's love for him,
Of his resurrection half the year.

Stars

July 2016

I lie between my children as they sleep,
I hold their legs,
it steadies something in me
and keeps them
from flying out the window at night.

If I had lamb's blood to mark the door,
I would.

What do you do these days,
the old rites are gone,

The stars lean in,
our ancestors say
only something new will save us.

Not only

July 2016

*(After I shared the above poem with my mentor Fran Quinn, he said, "Not **only**-tell us more, try to visualize what it is, that something new that will save is.)*

I'm listening

I don't know if it's terrible,
but I know something is there
trying to get my attention
or just seeing how stupid faithful I am

still trying to listen
with everything I have
and will an organ into existence that doesn't even exist yet
but which I seem to need
to receive

I continue to sleep with the
windows open
I try to stay awake for
as long as I can

leaning into the night
and its source
afraid but willing
that thing to come.

Nota Bene

(These are messages I have left for myself in the places I create. Some on post-it's, some on pages of journals, in the margins of creative projects, and others I have even painted on my walls. I have found them helpful, maybe your creative spirit will also be buoyed by my personal graffitti, too!)

1. Act as if guided—on everything.

2. Stop thinking so much—
    just do,
    clearheaded,
    with the clear poet beneath,
    the clear-feeling artist to guide you.

3. Find the clear line,
    click in,
    let the noise drown out all around you
    and let yourself be drawn
    by the greater pull
    the tone
    of the clear line.

4. Stop confusing "doubting" for thinking,
   and judging for creating.
   Keep the channel open,
   trust what comes,
   follow it, flow it.

5. NO WRONG MOVES
   NO WRONG MARKS
   (this was written two feet tall, in blue paint, on my old studio wall)

6. Relax.
   Relax your insides. Relax your outsides. Let the air surrounding you relax. Let the world relax.

Summer Night Storm

I'm tucked in bed in the corner bedroom in our family's old farmhouse in Rudd. I love this house and I love whoever built this house over a hundred and twenty years ago. I love the thunderstorm moving in. First distant rumbling thunder then closer splits the night. Now the rain. The sounds. I love the rain, the rain on the eaves, on the gutter through the gutter, on the windows, on the leaves of the trees. A lone cricket. I feel the house hold me and settle.

If I could write poetry
the way sleeping a night
in the farmhouse during a summer storm feels—
the world would be well.
The world that reads my words would be well.
There is wellness in this old house.
There is wellness in the falling rain.
There is wellness in these sounds.

Hungry

The kind of poetry I am most
hungry to read
is my own.

What follows next is a few revisions of a poem and my notes from rethinking this after conversations with my mentor Fran. Part of not just writing the poetry but viewing them as actually holding wisdom for me (and hopefully beyond me, too) is looking to what they are suggesting I do.

The vision I had for this poem was that it is time, past time, for me to move beyond hoarding the visions (and revisions) because I fear that they are not good enough or not wanted. I think the alchemist element that is still missing in this poem as it stands has something to do with releasing it now, as is.

The Rose

("The Rose" is the first draft I wrote, April 2016. "For Giving" is the next revision.)

The heavy ache in my chest for so long
a big black block
a brick
of coal

I realized all the flowers (they were roses) I hadn't been giving away
because they weren't good enough
I didn't know if you'd understand them
so I held them in,
held them so tight
my body clenched around them
and the pressure turned them
to coal

but now I've been burning that coal
and from the ashes
roses grow.

This time I'm giving them all away.

For Giving

That dark weight I felt in my chest
I looked to see
a black rock, like coal—
but more dense, like obsidian—
made of all the roses
I hadn't given away

I kept them, not for myself
not for you.
They were not for giving.
I didn't know if you'd want them anyway—

So I held them in,
my heart wrapped tightly around them,
closed in on itself,
un/for/giving.

That hand that should've been giving
instead was clenching,
holding on for dear life,
but crushing any chance of it.

But I breathed the other day,

like I haven't breathed in so long,
maybe decades,
and felt—
an unfurling.

This time I'm giving it all away.

*I would love to have versions of other poets' works along with notes about
their process! I learn so much from others' finished works, but what I
always feel is missing is a sense that they were ever in this place I so often
find myself. Where I receive the initial vision and then wade out into
unknown territory. I would love to be privy to the mind and process of
other creatives as they are IN process and before they have the security
of a "completed" work. Along those times, here are my notes on creative
process here after meeting with Fran Quinn:*

Hovering close to creation not the thing created.

*When you're getting a vision, you don't keep it vague. You keep it
specific. In that specificity you find it's collecting everything you need.*

*The "You" has also got to be something specific.
Try to get it more specific, then it will start to be more.*

Make the YOU more specific—let the imagination keep going with it.

So revision to get more specific...
Right at the beginning of a vision here...
Who is it that you're not going to give this to?
And is there some reason you're not giving it?
Who is it that you're not allowed to show that to?
Who is the YOU and why am I holding it back?
Or is it a YOU just because you've been taught not to do this?

Notes on motifs:

The rose is both spiritual and sexual—it has implications all over the place.

If this is Mary the Rose, feminine divine, and I'm choosing this, what am I doing?

If it is creative, sexual energy, and I'm choosing this, what am I doing?

How did it go from mineral life to vegetative life?

Allow yourself the vision. Then go back and re-vision it. Then start asking the questions-
Who is the You? What is the rose?

There is a big leap between line 4 & 5. What is at play there is alchemical.

Two of the three colors for alchemy are present – black and red. Now white should be there.

What is the transference out of stone energy into flower energy...

Apparition in the Mirror

Was it like
that time
    I saw myself in
     the mirror.
I didn't recognize myself but
I did.

Was that me?—

or was that me—

    the woman I
    looked up and caught

for a moment in the bathroom mirror
in San Diego—

    a memory of who
I thought I could be—and
was—for a moment—

Had I almost forgotten her?

Or is she the one
who startles me—

the lioness
who rises up
in the lower right corner
of the white blank room.

Where is that still pool where
I can really
see—

if I caught a clear vision—I too
might never look away.
Who is rattling
the cage of my chest and wanting
out.

After I'd written the first poem, I felt like it was asking for more. Not necessarily for more within that same poem, but that I get down more of the vision and that the "more" could become an accompaniment to the original version. This is the "more" in its current, raw form.

Apparition in the Mirror

Revision. September 15, 2013.

The face I saw
     stark stony reminding me of the boulders in the Sedona desert
although I hadn't been there yet, I recognized them when I ran
through the desert.
They sent off the same vibrating-silence-charge -
pounding, pulsing
 sentinels
       doves.

Heavy, immovable, stone doves
the weight of which I can't get off my shoulders.
The resounding silence,
the deep pulse of the earth
of silence and darkness
rising up and being discharged, encased,

I saw my face.
    Not for what my whole life I've been trying to see,
wanting to see,

something fell away between us

and she looked back at me,

and she stood, there, stationary (stationless), immobile, immovable,
   like those boulders
      or sentinels
and though I moved back and forth, like a skittering but fettered
mouse
she stood still
fierce and substance and with that stony face
and commanded I look at her (me) and see
the sheer blunt, raw, unfettered, force and strength and power in the
face, razor gaze
  I felt small in her presence

Something about seeing her made me go blank,
or I had to go blank in order to see her,

and in that blank and emptying that must happen
a sheer rock, stony face
a wielding gaze   timeless   primal?   if the soul appeared in a
face of rock
fierce, but not human fierce,
savage
the soul, raw and uncalculating,
clear as the wind, a force
everything emptied out in that moment to preserve me-
and in that space I got to see something normally hidden from sight,
something that lives beneath this world, some energy that dwells in the
bedrock, closer to the pulse, I felt that the only reason our
images matched in the mirror was because I wanted to be still
so she and the experience didn't slip away and the veil of normal
slip back
over everything—I felt that if I moved, she would have still held still—

and I felt I was gaining something in her presence
even though all things had fallen away
something was being added
it felt like she was emitting something palpable
something through her, something through the earth,
the boulders too I felt wiped clean
I was not big enough to contain it, so many parts had to be
broken and fall away and die, it was not so much a transfer of
energy—
or was it--but being in her presence I experienced something, and
being the boulders presence, I experienced something from them—
an emanation of
great silence, that cleans, purifies, it felt like being
immersed from the inside-out—like I was collecting, flooded through
with energy.

and tiger, lion- what do you have to do with this?
what role do you play?
Are you there to carry me back to the desert?
I've been wanting to go back
ever since I experienced those
giant boulders like doves
on the shoulders of the earth
to experience silence and depth and vastness
        and its message to the world
heal and heal

heal
        an ancient word
        a word that is a river
        a word that conveys
        a word that is a blessing
        cleans, indiscriminate   vague   true

a word that frees, unleashes

when I asked the tiger and lion if they are healers
they answered,
      we protect, we can't heal
      we deliver by consuming
      and sometimes we destroy to transform

words can't come to this place

The Wave

March 2016

Do you feel that?
        That wave coming
that sense of overwhelm
    You must let go
     And let yourself bob to the top
rise up with the tide
be carried with it
    learn to hold your breath
    with a calm mind

maybe you will grow gills.

Maybe you will rise to the top and
    Time after time of the wave tossing you

You will spread your arms and the wind
Will catch you and throw you up

Then you'll be able to soar
    plunge down again
    into the sea
    and fish and be as the fish

and rise up again   — no more limits for you.

no more limits.

the horizon is no longer a boundary
     only a fine line between earth and sky
     and you live everywhere and breathe.

Home

When all the landmarks are gone
and the people fading away,

When everything I called home
is falling,
going back into the Earth—

I'm tempted to believe decay
is worse than a plague.

I'm tempted to think it's
indifference.

I'm tempted to think
She
does not care and never did—

Except that I cannot shake
(even after all these years)
that memory—
 of lying, outstretched, in a snowy field,

and feeling
the gentle rise and fall
of Her breathing beneath me

as the grey sky, in it's great big quiet,
gave away
everything.

Façade

I can feel it so clearly sometimes,
and it seems almost funny.

A woman,
average height,
average build,
nice smile,

What an interesting choice of façade
For the infinite black and starry, starry night.

Closer Than Breath

Now and then I forget
but,

                                  Beneath the noise of all my trying to become,
lies the deep stillness of who I am

Closer than breath.

This Is How You Move Through Walls

October 2014

There, again, was the wall.

But still I tried.

This time it was the strength of my heartbreak and longing
This time,
a declaration, a promise,

That it is me or the wall,

The strength of my desire colliding with that God-forsaken wall –
worse yet than
God-forsaken- a God-planted longing in me colliding moving toward
the music it
hears colliding with a God-built wall, so impenetrable, so infinite
that there is no
room left to believe that He meant for me to break it down or go
around—and yet
so strong is the desire to go through...

That I can no longer stay on this side without carving out a piece of

my heart,
(The part I love so much, that part that hears the music and will not
let me stop
dancing towards it)–

just so I can be at peace, not go crazy, not die from heartbreak. On
this side of the

wall, a half-life or insanity.

But there still is the wall.

I have sent up too many prayers over the years and heard a variety of
answers –

Go over, around, break it down, go through...

They sound clever, maybe clever enough if this was a different kind
of wall, but all

rang hollow.

This last time the answer was different.

This time it had the unmistakable, mysterious tone of truth,
a resonance I could feel before
I could move it to my mind
and before my mind could move it to words, it rang--

This is how you move through walls.

Give up everything you thought real.

Make yourself unreal,

Like water, let everything hard in you melt into fluid, become water—
But less physical yet—
Let the water vanish into thin air—
But less yet—
The air vanish into spirit,
But you don't vanish,

You make yourself as unlike the wall as possible
Let all your own inner walls crumble,
Let go of trying to hold together your life and your physical form.
This is how you move through walls—
Not with force
But by giving up
Everything in you that you thought was real,
Everything
That is hard and unbelieving.

This is how you move through walls, unbroken.

A Long Rope

November 28, 2014

I am thinking this morning
of my sisters in Afghanistan—

the invisible ones who must write their landays on the air.

While my heart pounds
from fear of being caught
or the exhilaration of being alive

I am:

waiting for silence, or
waiting for the cover of noise,
waiting

to draw the curtains back from my mouth
so that I may trace the forms of my days (too straight for my heart)
and carve the shape of it,
with words, with sound,
with my voice--
into the ears of my sisters and daughter.

So that I may attempt
To make meaning from my days
And make my day's meaning

While you...

Drop it straight from the mouth of a fierce and unforgiving God
Whose mercy is to give you no veil, no chance for pretend meaning

Pain and slavery have liberated your lips
Your voice came into existence wailing
And no comforts have been added since then
To soften the sharp terror edge of your voice
Only
Mixed the blood with dirt and desert sand and ground,
Burned your voice into a silvery thing
Made of your tongue a sharp and curved blade
That glints

And slices

A nimble whip
That cracks and flicks through the air

These words can be nothing more special to you
Than air
So might as well use them
As you might as well breathe

You know so much better than we

We who are "free"...
have the illusion that Death waits for us, maybe because Death is just

further removed in our case
And therefore seems so much more controllable, submissive to our manipulations

And negotiations

Where, the slave who is also free, knows Death could be your father, could be your brother, your husband...Death could be your friend

Waiting, you know, is the senseless murderer

You would no sooner wait to loosen your heart, your tongue,
Than you would wait to breathe...

While we, who are breathing just a little and calling it a life,
Breathe just a little, wait, and call it a life...

These words can be nothing more special to you
Than air

These words
These words
Sharp and jagged
And deadly as knives
Cut bread
Draw blood
Leave scars or
Make the final wound

But the cut that is most deadly
Is the small and slow one
The one we barely notice
The wound we carve in the heart

With our waiting, it's a slow blood letting and such a slow death
We hardly notice

The slow cut
The one we barely notice
The one that relieves a little pressure
Lets a little blood
But lets us go on existing,
The one that is just the fleeting, almost imperceptible little shock
That keeps us in our places, we hardly even notice it,
We imagine we imagine it,
But it keeps us shut up and in our places

The one that,
Gradually, layer after layer of hardened and deadened tissue
Numbs and deadens our ability to taste the world, to kiss,
To speak

It's the cut that keeps our hearts hidden, trapped beneath the scarred
tissue in our chests, instead of rising through our throats and singing
to the world

It keeps our bodies moving along our straight and known
Paths,
Bedroom to bathroom, bedroom to kitchen,
Kitchen to office, to school to store to work
(and we think we gained liberation by moving to work but we just
added another straight line)

when what we are built for is to dance,
naked,
all over the goddamn place and on the tables and rooftops and
mountain tops and strip mall parking lots.

Every time we wait—
    One more cut
Until our tongues grow numb and thick

No longer sharp and nimble
Like a curved blade
Slicing the ear
Carving the swiftest arc to God's ear

While we are our own slow and silent killers,
Crippling ourselves,
Moving in our straight lines,
Back and forth,

Meanwhile longing for the dance
But the music we are waiting to hear never comes, never moves us—
Because we have buried the drums and starved the bird--

But deepest is the wound to the world

Silence

Where voices could be ringing out—
Praise, lament, grief, rejoicing, birth, agony, death, pain, and
pleasure

Or simply—

I am here.

Everywhere
we are sending our pails
down

into the well.

All of us
hoping to draw up
meaning
that will sustain us all—

So if you, all my anonymous sisters,
happen to find yourself
Parched
And in a place that seems God-forsaken—
Beneath a burning sun,
trapped in a violent desert storm,
or in a big box called Target with very small and pissed-off children—
(thinking you have nothing worth writing about)...

Do not give up!
Do not die of thirst because you begin to doubt water—
Doubt that it's there,
Doubt that it was ever there—

Keep lowering your pail
Into the depths of these ordinary things
For it is sometimes in things that seem the shallowest, most
mundane, and ordinary
When you need...

just know you'll need
an extra,
extra
long
rope.

Song of Self

The self comes through the song
if you don't sing, you haven't really yet
come into being...

To come alive go outside

Don't forget the life that lives
outside
the capture of the frame.

Creative Prompt:

Meditations for Your Imagination.

For all of these prompts, there are two guidelines:

1. Use your imagination to play with these prompts, work with
    them, and engage with them with all of your faculties (physical,
    emotional, spiritual, mental, energetic).

2. Until you feel a shift, an opening.

This is one of the ways I think of breaking through to that, "Wild Blue
Yonder," that place where I am a clear, non-self-conscious, and fully
present channel for expression and there are limitless possibilities!
Many times, often times (especially in the beginning), it's like you
only get a little "whiff" of this energetic shift—but that is enough! I
like to think of that as a portal opening to that Wild Blue Yonder and
once the portal has been opened, once you've felt that, you can find
your way back. You can retrace your steps and practice until you can
do it again, access that new feeling state, that new way of being, and
practice holding it longer and longer and longer— until it becomes
such a predominant part of your experience that it becomes your
new reality. Where you once used to force because you didn't trust
and you were trying to compensate, you relax and settle back into

your ease and innate power. And then worlds within and without open to you and you to them. Remember—the openings absolutely exist. The way you find them is such an exquisite part of your creative process and strengthens you in embodying the creative force of nature that you have always been.

PROMPT 1: Falling into Place

Imagine...

The feeling of everything

falling into place.

I love to use this prompt to guide me into a place of ease and flow when I am creating. Even when I am doing something that requires a high degree of engagement from me, I find asking my imagination to meditate upon what it would be like, in mind, body, and spirit, to be engaged in a process where everything is falling into place. The prompt, "the feeling of everything falling into place," seems to be a very effective order that all parts of me understand—the parts that need to quiet and settle down do, the parts that need to awaken and engage do, and I get to step into a dance with something bigger than me: That Which Wants To Happen.

I also like to use this prompt in tandem with the next.

_____

_____

_____

_____

PROMPT 2: Settle & Surrender

This is an Imagination Meditation I love to practice when things are going wonderfully, when I'm feeling a little off or lost or unsure of a next step, and also at times when I'm feeling really lost and like nothing I am doing is working. I feel it brings both my soul, my perspective, and my imagination back into a sense of Connection with Creativity and proper alignment and focus.

So, use this in good times—it just feels amazing AND it's also best to sew your parachute and keep this connection strong before you find yourself mid-free fall!

Also, use this if:

- You find yourself wanting desperately to create and you can't seem to get out of your own way

- You feel stuck in the fight-flight-or-freeze responses of Survival Mode

- You are burned out

- You are working so hard but everything feels forced and nothing Is falling into place.

Sometimes this technique will help you completely downshift into Creative Mode, other times it will just make you realize where your suffering and burden and forcing is created by trying to do that which is not yours. Sometimes it will allow you to see the next tiny step in front of you that is yours to take. That, though small, can still feel like such a huge relief. And those tiny steps still put you squarely back into alignment with Creativity, which is a huge miracle.

STEP 1   Put both hands on your heart. Close your eyes. Breathe deeply. Relax the outer and inner parts of you.

STEP 2   Remaining still and continuing to breathe deeply, call to mind a specific, current creative work you are engaged with. For example, it can be looking at your week ahead full of work commitments, household chores, and family commitments; it could be the current stage of a beautiful creative dream or vision you have for your life that you are currently working on. It could be a pattern that challenges you in a relationship. This can be applied to any area of your life.

STEP 3   Ask yourself:

What is mine here?

What is not mine here?

What part of any confusion, block, suffering, exhaustion, forcing, overwhelm I am experiencing is being created by me trying to take on what is not mine to take on?

STEP 4   Settle into what is yours, release what is not. Feel the truth of what is yours, notice how, even if it requires effort and courage, it never feels beyond you. Settle into that, be grateful for what is yours. And perhaps repeat to yourself, "I am feeling burdened/overwhelmed/

confused because I am trying to take on what is not mine to take on. I am aware of that now and I release what is not mine. I release over-functioning, overreaching and settle into the truth and power of knowing what is mine, owning that, and releasing anything that is not that.

STEP 5 Just notice any shifts, notice how you feel, notice any new insights and steep in that, breathing deeply. Then rise and go about what is yours.

PROMPT 3: On Resistance

On Resistance

I used to mistake myself for Resistance all the time. Learning to slow down and feel into my

mind and body, learning to slow down and acknowledge that the greater part of me is this creative force that wants to flow is flowing, is clear, always connected, and true was a great liberation and turning point for me.

And still, sometimes I forget. Sometimes I still get myself so tangled up and enmeshed in the

Resistance that I forget that, "underneath all that I am trying to become is the greater force of

who I already am, closer than breath." Sometimes I still mistake myself for the Resistance.

But if I am feeling that, I can slow down and ask, "Am I mistaking myself for Resistance here?"

Sometimes there is an immediate shift, sometimes a tiny opening. But even that small opening can help me remember, "I am not the Resistance," and it opens my awareness to reconnect with the greater force of who I really am.

I have found my clients, too, may often lapse into this amnesia where they suffer from forgetting their greatness and, instead, their self-concept is also enmeshed with Resistance. If you ever find yourself here, try these simple steps:

1. Get quiet, take some deep breaths, and bring yourself to stillness. Then bring your awareness to the interior of your mind and your body. Just notice what you notice there. Explore. Rather than lumping yourself into one generalized experience, can you notice nuances and differences within yourself? Borders of certain feelings? Tension in some areas, expansiveness, openness in others?

1. If you feel any signs of Resistance, any tension, anything that feels "not you," remind yourself that you are not alone in confusing yourself with Resistance.

2. Can you tell if your awareness is hyper-focused on a certain area and/or very wound up in another? If so, do you notice elsewhere in your experience where this is not the case? Expand your focus and awareness to take in the entirety of you (Or try! You may find you sense you have no borders!) rather than the hypervigilance and over-identification with one specific area or experiential phenomenon.

3. Notice where you do feel anything that feels like Resistance. Allow it and also allow yourself to expand your focus to not be bound in it, but to be so vast as to easily, easily hold it and with plenty of room to spare.

4. Ask yourself, "What is the greater force of who I am?" See if you can feel into that.

5. Ask yourself, "Am I mistaking myself for Resistance?" And if so, gently release anything, including Resistance, that is not you. The Resistance doesn't have to leave, but you also do not have to clutch it tightly in the talons of your focus.

6. Send gratitude to your current experience and the call to stillness and the invitation to reconnect. Rather than feeling down about this happening, be grateful for the phenomenon and use it as an invitation to reconnect with the expansive truth of who you really are.

PROMPT 4: Six Impossible Things

Six Impossible Things

"Alice laughed: "There's no use trying," she said; "**one can't believe impossible things**." *"I daresay you haven't had much practice,"* said *the Queen. "When I was younger, I always did it for half an hour a day. Why, sometimes I've* **believed** *as many as* **six impossible things before breakfast.**"

LEWIS CARROLL, ALICE IN WONDERLAND

This is another Imagination Meditation I love to practice at all times and it was inspired by the quote above from that creative genius, Lewis Carroll, and his magical work of art, Alice in Wonderland.

I love coming up with new ways for my clients and me to exercise and strengthen our believe-ability muscles and Believing 6 Impossible Things Before Breakfast is one of my favorite workouts to recommend for that purpose!

This is another practice I love for when things are wonderful, when they are dark and heavy, or maybe I'm just feeling "meh." It brings an infusion of the energy of possibility, joy, delight, fun, and surprise into my life...and all before I've even had my second cup of coffee with breakfast!

I love to do this especially when moving, for instance outside for a walk or run or on my Peloton. I also love it as a stream of consciousness journaling exercise or in a seated meditation! Experiment with how you love to access the energy of believing the impossible and have fun! And when your analytical brain tries to fly in and play the role of Alice here (as well as Debbie Downer) by telling you, "But that's impossible!"

And you have a very pat answer ready for it, "That's right, Captain Obvious. I already said that— these are 'impossible' things, so I don't need to do the part of trying to figure out how they could happen in a logical universe."

Also, if we parse it out, there are two very specific pieces of wisdom in the Queen's response. First, the secret from moving from the realm of impossible to BELIEVING is an available option in itself. Second, the key to moving from impossible into BELIEVING in the impossible is PRACTICE. Not just considering it once, twice, but practicing it. She even prescribes 30 minutes a day, at the start of the day.

The whole point of this is to stretch your imagination, mind, body, and spirit to belief that which yet seems illogical, irrational, impossible. Once stretched and strengthened in this way, a funny thing happens... things that once seemed impossible either serve you because, 1. You delight yourself so much with this make-believe (i.e., MAKE BELIEF) exercise, and/or 2. Those rules you once thought were hard and fast about what is possible for you and what is not begin to shift. The realm of what's possible for you seems less constrained by logic and more designed by the architecture of your imagination, the stretch and strength of it.

Note: Remember Imagination Meditation Guideline #2! Practice this, as the Queen says, and practice this until you feel a shift! And then keep going practicing feeling those shifts in beliefs until you see the shifts in your world – things that once were impossible become part of your waking reality!

Believe 6 impossible things before breakfast...

Imagine, every day before breakfast,

6 different scenarios, all which your rational brain currently declare to be impossible.

Turn them over with your imagination and feel into what it would be like to believe, REALLY BELIEVE, that these impossible things were your reality.

How would you feel? How would you be different? What would life be like? What would you be thinking? Not thinking? What would you do differently? What does the energy of totally believing this feel like? What different emotions/states can you access with this exercise?

It can also be great to write these down in your journal. Maybe you have the same 6 everyday for a while, maybe a different six, maybe half and half.

Marinate in the energy of the possibility of the impossible in your life! Maybe you can only do it for three minutes at first, but maybe you stretch that to 30, and then maybe it takes. On a life of it's own and new potentials and possibilities begin showing up in your life.

Finally, a fun, provocative question I love to ask at the end of this exercise:

What would I have to believe in order for this to be obvious and natural for me instead of impossible right now?

PROMPT 5: Prayers Are Answered

Live as if your prayers are answered.

I'm laughing as I write this because this is one I'm practicing right now! One of my prayers is to live as a creative force of nature, an artist who is a channel for a Creativity and who believes that that work comes to good, an artist that trusts the process of creating from a soulful place and honors That Which Wants To Happen, even when the first (and second and third...) attempts make her analytical and style sensibilities cringe. For a long, long time, I have been obsessed with the creative genius of others. I realize that that is in part because I want to be one. And when I dive deep into that, into why I want that, I always come to the same conclusion. It is because I believe creative geniuses are entitled to trust their ideas and are entitled to honor the work they create—even the "bad" ideas and the work that seems not yet to be anything remarkable. A creative genius is entitled to be curious and fascinated by their own ideas, to wonder more about "What is working in this, what thing is trying to be born here and come to life?" than they ever give time to questioning, "Am I wasting my time? Why am I not better yet? This is so bad it'll embarrass me." A creative genius is allowed to trust themselves, to believe in Creativity and the infinite wisdom, genius, beauty, and profound meaning unfolding through being engaged in a creative way of life.

Here is how I suggest using this particular Imagination mediation:

1. Call to mind a prayer of yours.

2.   Imagine it is answered. It may help if you first envision a scene from your life, like a scene from a movie, out in front of you that illustrates you living in this life after this prayer has been answered. Watch, observe a while. Notice what's different. Notice what is the same. And then, once you have this scene in your mind, move into the scene. Merge with the you whose prayers have been answered. Be in his/her body. See through her/his eyes. Feel how you feel, this self whose prayers have been answered. Notice how you no longer feel. Notice what you are thinking. Notice what you are no longer thinking. Notice what you desire to focus on in your life and how you desire to be, *who you allow yourself to be* as this person whose prayers have been answered. Breathe deeply and steep in that energy. Feel how it feels to be in your mind, body, spirit in this "prayers answered paradigm."

3.   What you are doing in step 2 is meditating, meditating in the sense that you are becoming familiar with the way of being, which I believe is the essence of what you truly desire and which I also believe is the energy which helps us create the external reality we feel best suits us, because we have created it from the inside out. Step 2, where you are imagining the scene is giving you a mirror for you to understand how you wish to be on the inside. In turn, once you practice (meditate upon, become familiar with holding) this state of being on the inside, it allows you to create from an entirely different place.

I do think this is a way I practice "moving through walls" as I was describing in the earlier poem. I have experienced that feeling of being walled off from my artist self that channels creativity and flows it through to completion at various times in my life. I've learned to move through those walls with imagination meditations just as the one I've just shared. Right now, as I write this book, I'm learning to move through another. My ego would prefer I tidy the process up before attempting a book, but when I leaned into what my inner Creative Guide and Guardian, my Creative Genius, had to say, they said, "this

is how you move through this wall. Through the writing of this book."
And I am living as someone whose prayers are answered, who is a
creative genius and is allowed to trust and honor her work and her
process at all stages, by writing this words to you now.

_____

_____

_____

_____

_____

_____

_____

_____

_____

_____

_____

_____

_____

PROMPT 6: Walking into Your Dreams

Walking into the life of your dreams.

Movement, for me, is such an essential part of creativity. And while I cannot yet prove it and am only relying on my own experience, anecdotal stories of my clients and other creative geniuses who used movement as a part of their process, and relatively recent scientific research, I'll just dare to go out on a limb and say I think movement can be a master key for unlocking new levels of creative genius for anyone.

Here is an Imagination Mediation that you can use with many of the other practices I've shared in this book.

This is how you take your dreams for a walk as a way of walking into the life of your dreams:

Consider a dream you have. Choose one specific thing to focus on that will be a part of your living, breathing, waking life once this dream has become a reality. It could be a thought (for example, *I am a published author!*) or it could be a scene (*you're holding the book in your hands! Or opening your first royalty check! Or your best friends and family are hugging you, saying congratulations on the wonderful, wonderful book and that they are so amazed and proud of you!*).

What I want you to do next is study your future self, the self that has created the dream and is living in the dream. What is really important is that you don't go into problem solving mode trying to figure out how she did it at this point. You stay firmly in the energy of IT IS DONE, YOU HAVE DONE IT!

Then, as best you can for the entire walk, you place this scene in your heart and mind and do everything you can imagine to conjure the energy in your heart and mind that matches what you feel the energy of this scene is. You focus all of your attention for the entire walk, telling yourself, I WILL feel this, I AM going to open this portal in this walk, I'm going to feel and and it's going to feel so very, very real that it moves me.

I will sometimes write a symbol or note on my hand to remind me to focus. Or I will carry a notecard with a symbol of this dream on it. The notecard requires some attention to continue to carry and can help remind me when my mind wanders. And your mind WILL wander. A good deal of energy in this practice is about training your mind to focus on a single intention for an extended period of time and so intently so that you actually feel as if you've been out for a walk in the future. Some day in the future, when you've created the dream, you will also go out for a walk. Today, as you're creating the dream, you also take walks. Somewhere in the middle, these two versions of you will rendezvous if you make it your unbending intent for that to be the case as you go on these walks and contemplate all the amazing possibilities for your life!

Closing

Albert Einstein said, "Logic will get you from A to B. Imagination will take you everywhere."

Just imagine! Wherever you dream of going...your imagination can take you there!

If you ever find yourself in a place where you are feeling disheartened, discouraged, stuck, or lost, I would invite you to remember that one doesn't experience these kind of more frustrating energies of Resistance without there being a very great counter-force of a creativity that wants to flow at work. The tension we can experience as creatives can be intense, so take extraordinary care of yourself, trust yourself, and see if you can relax into the greater force of What Wants to Happen through you. Ask for guidance and you will receive it.

I hope I have shared some such guidance with you in these pages, but even more than the poems and the prompts, what I most want to impart to you is that your dream is there for a reason, you ARE built to be a creative genius and a force of nature for good, and, at the end of the day, you are doing a great job and you will always, always be deeply okay.

In closing, I hope this little book, these poems and these prompts, help you on your own Wild, Blue Yonder adventure, your own journey to the everywhere you could ever imagine, and quite possibly beyond as well.

Acknowledgements

I want to thank my dear little family.

Brad – you are a wonderful husband and partner in so many of my life's greatest adventures. Thank you for your relentless, amazing love and support and your own inspiring dedication to becoming the greatest, most loving version of yourself as a person, a father, a husband, a friend, and a teacher.

To Elijah, Samuel, and Blaise – you are proof that the Wild Blue Yonder is real. You are proof and reason for living as someone who knows, with their whole heart and soul, that this is a world made for believing in your dreams, for giving, for growing, for miracles, for love, and for always the possibility of falling more deeply in love than you ever imagined possible.

I could never make it to my dreams without you. I love you all so much.

I also want to thank you, dear reader. If you were inspired to pick up this book, I'm willing to bet that you have a powerful, beautiful dream on the horizon and that your own inner guide is leading you to all that you need to support yourself in the creation of that vision. When gorgeous, creative geniuses like you follow their heart and souls, magic happens – in your own life and it spills out into the world. So from the bottom of my creative heart and soul – thank you. You are making the world a better place with every step you take.

Bio

Leah Campbell Badertscher, J.D. is an artist, writer, and master life and creativity coach. She is the founder of Renascence Co, The Art School, and The Art School Podcast. She lives on a farm in Michigan with her husband, three children, 16 chickens, Izzy the cat, and Luna, the golden doodle.

Learn more at www.leahcb.com or contact her at support@leahcb.com.